Land of the Free

10 Patriotic Piano Solos
by Carolyn Mille

T0210298

ISBN 978-1-4234-0912-0

EXCLUSIVELY DISTRIBUTED BY

WILLIS MUSIC

HAL•LEONARD®
CORPORATION
7777 W. BLUEMOUND RD. P.O. BOX 13819
MILWAUKEE, WISCONSIN 53213

In Australia contact:
Hal Leonard Australia Pty. Ltd.
4 Lentara Court
Cheltenham, Victoria, 3192 Australia
Email: ausadmin@halleonard.com

Visit Hal Leonard Online at
www.halleonard.com

My Country, 'Tis of Thee
(America)

Words by Samuel Francis Smith
Music from *Thesaurus Musicus*
Arranged by Carolyn Miller

Moderato

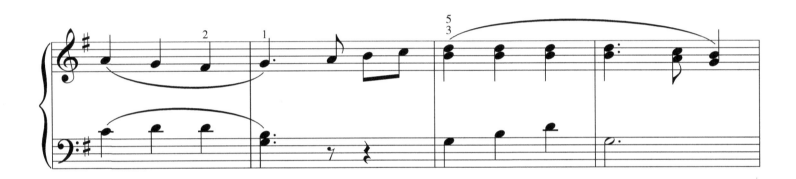

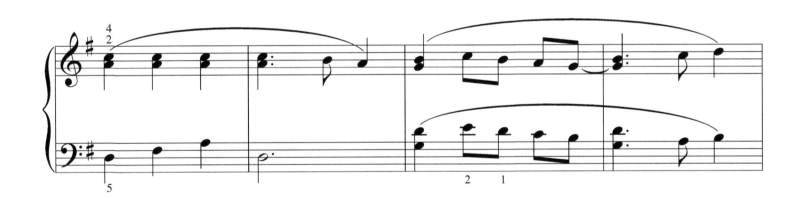

The Caissons Go Rolling Along

Words and Music by Edmund L. Gruber
Arranged by Carolyn Miller

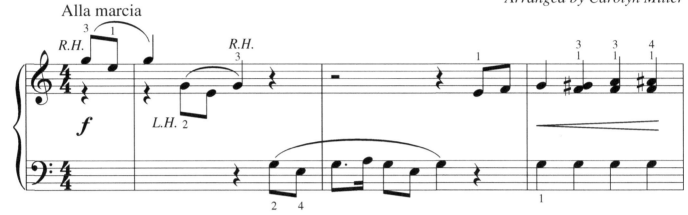

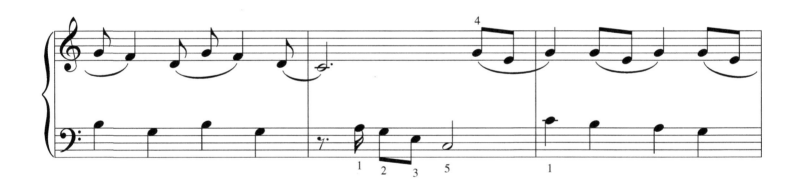

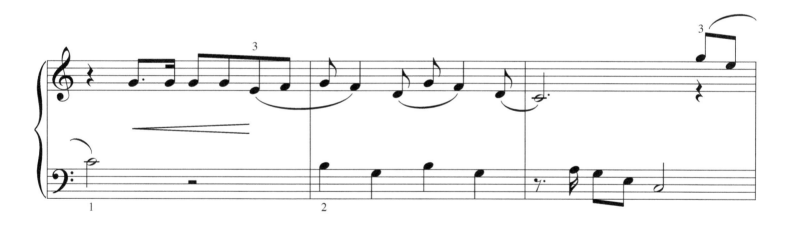

The Star Spangled Banner

Words by Francis Scott Key
Music by John Stafford Smith
Arranged by Carolyn Miller

Yankee Doodle

Traditional
Arranged by Carolyn Miller

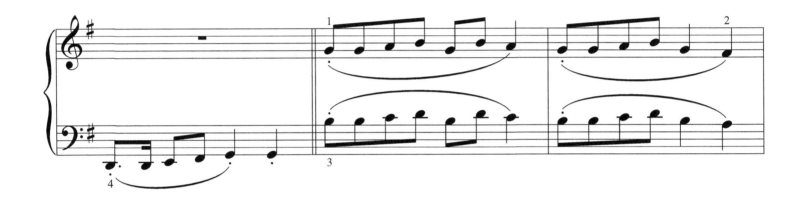

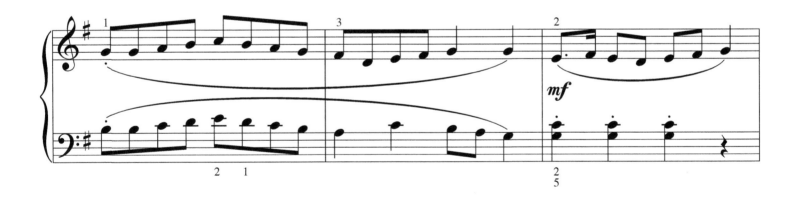

(I Wish I Was In)
Dixie

Words and Music by Daniel Decatur Emmett
Arranged by Carolyn Miller

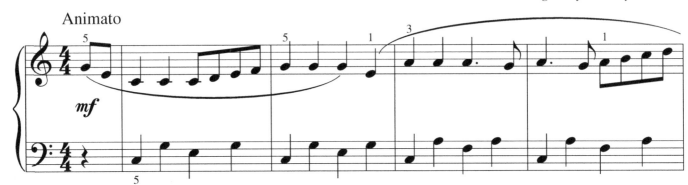

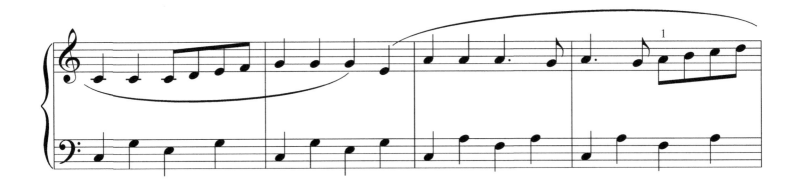

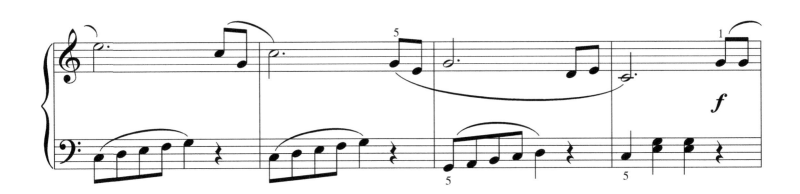

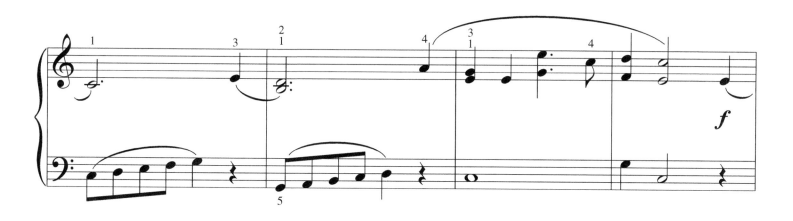

Slower   A tempo

America, the Beautiful

Words by Katherine Lee Bates
Music by Samuel A. Ward
Arranged by Carolyn Miller

Moderato

Marine's Hymn

Words by Henry C. Davis
Melody based on a theme by Jacques Offenbach
Arranged by Carolyn Miller

The American Patrol

By F.W. Meacham
Arranged by Carolyn Miller

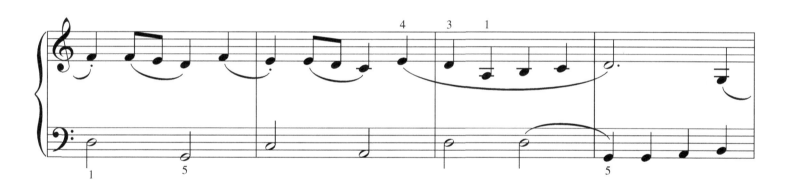

Battle Hymn of the Republic

Words by Julia Ward Howe
Music by William Steffe
Arranged by Carolyn Miller

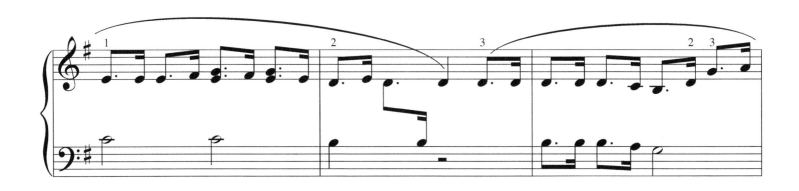

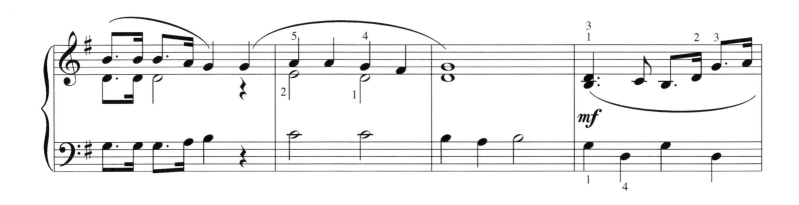

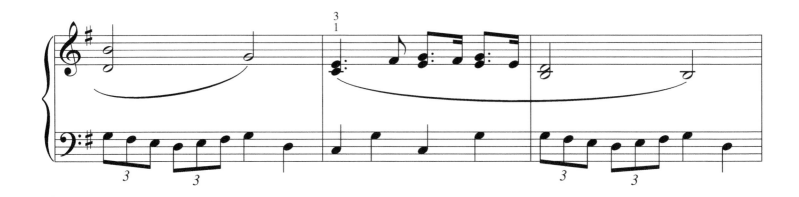

Stars and Stripes Forever

By John Philip Sousa
Arranged by Carolyn Miller

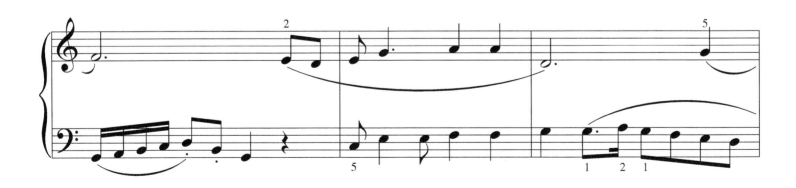